I Survived Trauma...
Now What?

A Humorous Guide to Sorting
Through the Wreckage

Bernice Walker MS, NCC

Disclaimer: This book uses humor as a tool for healing, not as a way to minimize or belittle trauma. Remember, healing is a personal journey and what works for one may not work for all. If you find yourself needing professional help, please reach out. Life is too short to walk through it without a decent road map (or at least some terrible dad jokes).

Dedication

The one who has always believed in me. I won't mention your name and embarrass you, but you know who you are...

Content

A Note from the Author.

This book is a testament to one core belief: no matter the chapter titles in your life, from "Wait, What?!" to "Seriously, Universe?!", you're the writer holding the pen. Each page you turn, each chapter you close, is your choice and your narrative.

But let's get one thing clear: while this book might be sprinkled with humor, the journey of trauma and recovery is anything but trivial. The fact that you're here, turning pages, seeking understanding, and maybe a giggle, shows immense courage. It shows that deep down, beneath the layers of doubt and pain, there's a resilience that shouts, "I'm still here, world. What's next?"

If there's one thing to take away it's this: never, ever give up. If trauma is a chapter (or ten) in your book, remember that you've got the whole rest of the story waiting to be written. Plot twists, cliffhangers, romantic subplots, and maybe even a space alien invasion – it's all up to you.

As you journey through these pages, I hope you find insight, laughter, and perhaps a few "Aha!" moments to add to your personal toolkit. After all, you're not just the main character; you're the hero of your tale.

So, let's dive in. Get ready to explore, to laugh, to ponder, and most importantly, to write your story with flair, wit, and perhaps just a smidge of confetti.

Introduction

Life's Wild Rollercoaster
(And No, You Can't Pick Your Seat)

Welcome, brave reader, to a whirlwind exploration of life, love, trauma, and the art of finding laughter in the most unexpected places. Have you ever felt like life is a game show where the rules keep changing, the prizes are perplexing, and the host speaks in riddles? You're not alone. Dive into these pages, where we navigate the unpredictable waters of existence, find solace in shared experiences, and, most importantly, learn that when life gives you pickles instead of lemons, it might just be time to make a sandwich. Buckle up, keep your arms and legs inside the narrative at all times, and let's embark on this unconventional journey together!

Chapter 1

....

"Did Life Just Give Me Lemons or Was That a Pineapple?"

Hey there, brave soul! If you've cracked open this guide, it's likely that life decided to play a game of darts with you. The catch? You were the dartboard. And man, life's aim was either impeccable or absolutely atrocious, because here you are. Welcome to the club - the "Did That Really Just Happen?" Society. We don't have matching T-shirts or secret handshakes, but we sure have a collection of jaw-dropping tales, cringe-worthy moments, and a shared love for humor-infused Band-Aids.

The "Life's Wild Rollercoaster" Ride

Joining the "Life's Wild Rollercoaster" ride wasn't on your bucket list, was it? Surprise! It's that amusement park you never asked for. Like being strapped into a ride that has more loops than you can count, with a seatbelt that feels suspiciously loose. But hey, the view from the top? Breathtaking. The company? Stellar.

Membership Perks (Disclaimer: Irony Ahead!)

This isn't your run-of-the-mill club. The perks? Unexpectedly delightful:

- **X-ray Vision:** Nah, not the superhero kind, but the ability to see through BS like you have a sixth sense. Others see a wall; you see the world's most obvious door.

- **MacGyver Instincts:** You've somehow developed the knack to get out of emotionally sticky situations using just a toothpick, some glitter, and your wits.

- **The Emotional Buffet:** A smorgasbord of feelings, from deep introspective moments to bouts of "I-can't-even". And a sprinkling of "Did I just laugh at that?"

Comedy: The Glow-in-the-Dark Band-Aid

Let's address the elephant in the room: Why do trauma and humor even belong in the same sentence? Imagine getting lost in a dense, dark forest (yep, the trauma). Now, humor is that trusty glow-in-the-dark band-aid you slap on every time you get pricked. It lights your path, offers some relief, and reminds you of a world outside where things are a tad less prickly.

Mapping the "What Now?" Terrain

Life post-whammy is less of a walk in the park and more of a climb up a hilariously unpredictable mountain named "What Now?". One moment it's sunny, the next it's raining marshmallows. Every peak scaled brings its share of chuckles, groans, and "I-can't-believe-I-just-did-that" tales.

Connecting Over Campfire Stories

The road to healing, while personal, is sprinkled with fellow adventurers, ready to swap stories over metaphorical campfires. Some have tumbled down rabbit holes, others have gone through wardrobes into snowy wonderlands, but all bring tales of resilience, a dash of chaos, and a heavy dose of comic relief.

Final Pit Stop (Or Just a Breather)

Steering ahead, Chapter 2 zooms into the maze called PTSD. Ever wondered why your brain plays reruns at the oddest times? Or why certain tunes give you dramatic movie flashbacks? We're cranking up the tunes and diving deep. Pedal to the metal, fellow traveler.

Chapter 2

PTSD: Not Just an Over-Priced Sandwich on the Menu

So, you've stumbled upon "PTSD", Post-Traumatic Stress Disorder. It's one of those acronyms that sound like it should be accompanied by a crisp white lab coat. It sounds formal and fancy, doesn't it? But if PTSD was a party guest, it would be the one who shows up uninvited, eats all the snacks, and stays way past its welcome. Let's dive deeper into this party pooper.

PTSD Unpacked: This Ain't No Party Favor

Sure, we know PTSD isn't exclusive to war veterans or action movie heroes. It's a bonus gift (sans gift receipt) for anyone who's endured trauma, like surviving the horrors of a blind date, or more seriously, an accident or personal loss.

Symptoms: Or What We Like to Call – Unexpected Party Tricks

Now, while dramatic flashbacks do make the list, there's a variety of other ways PTSD likes to jazz up your life:

- **Hyperarousal:** Where every creak, pop, or ding can make you jumpier than a cat on a hot tin roof.

- **Avoidance:** Ever tried to dodge someone you owed money to at a party? PTSD makes you dodge places, songs, or even Aunt Mildred.

- **Numbing:** It's like someone hit the mute button on your emotions.

- **Negative Thoughts:** Where you can sometimes be a little too hard on yourself, more than a food critic at a gas station sushi joint.

- **Intrusive Memories:** Your brain suddenly thinks it's a director and keeps replaying certain events over and over. Except it's not the fun memories like that time you ate the biggest ice cream cone, but the ones you'd rather not remember.

- **Distorted Blame:** It's playing the blame game, but the rules are all skewed. You might end up blaming yourself for things way out of your control. Like, "If only I hadn't worn those mismatched socks, everything would've been different."

- **Difficulty Concentrating:** Trying to focus becomes like trying to watch TV with someone else holding the remote. Channels keep changing, and just when you're getting into a show, BAM! You're watching an infomercial on potato peelers.

Triggers: Life's Nasty Little "Surprise! Gotcha!" Moments

For someone with PTSD, triggers are life's jack-in-the-boxes. Sometimes obvious, sometimes sneakier than a ninja in socks on a marble floor.

Coping Mechanisms: The Jigsaw Puzzles with a Few Missing Pieces

Everyone has their way of dealing with PTSD's curveballs. Some methods, like joining a dance class or therapy, are solid. Others, like pretending you're a potato, are a bit questionable. Remember, it's essential to separate the rock 'n' roll from the just plain "rocky".

Treatment: Let's Get Down to Brass Tacks

Now, therapy is the crown jewel here. Techniques with fancy names like EMDR and CBT – which, by the way, are not distant relatives of CBD (though that's an entirely different conversation).

The Mighty Power of Commune...ity!

They say it takes a village to raise a child. Well, it sometimes takes a community to heal a soul. Support groups are like those family reunions where everyone "gets it" (minus the awkward potato salad). Navigating the murky waters of trauma is a tad bit like attempting synchronized swimming in a kiddie pool – it's awkward, confounding, and you're fairly certain there's a better way to do it. Here's where support groups come into play. Think of them as your lifeline or that one trusty floatie that ensures you don't go nose-first into the shallow end. And no, these groups don't have to be about trauma. It's not a requirement for everyone to gather and discuss "that one event." It can be a club where everyone shares an inexplicable passion for interpretive dance or an appreciation group for '90s cartoon theme songs. The key isn't the topic; it's about finding a space where you can bond, share, and feel utterly connected to others. It's the difference between solo karaoke in your shower and belting out power ballads with a group of equally off-key enthusiasts. The theme is optional; the connection is essential. And who knows? You might discover you're not the only one who can recite every line from that obscure movie or believes pineapple has no place on pizza. The point is: find your tribe, embrace the shared vibe, and revel in the collective high-five!

Navigating the Rollercoaster

Diving into the world of PTSD is like being thrust onto a rollercoaster when you thought you were in line for the merry-go-round. First, there's the slow, anticipatory climb. You're learning, adjusting, gripping the safety bar a tad too tight, maybe regretting that large soda you had earlier. Then come the plunging descents into unexpected realizations, where your stomach does mini backflips, and you're fairly sure gravity's gone on a break. Don't even get me started on the loop-de-loops; those confusing moments that throw you for a loop, where you're not sure if you're coming, going, or if your hair's just permanently defying gravity now.

But here's the twist: amidst the dizzying drops and whirlwind turns, there are moments of clarity, where the view from the top is breathtaking and the breeze feels invigorating. And let's not forget the candid (often unflattering) snapshot at the ride's climax – a genuine reminder of the journey you've taken, wide-eyed expressions and all.

Most importantly, even amidst the rollercoaster's chaos, there's a structure, a path that's been designed with care. You've got your safety harness (your support system), fellow riders screaming alongside you (because who wants to scream alone?), and a track leading you forward. There might be jolts and jerks, but there's always an end in sight. And when it's over? You can look back, feel the thrill, appreciate the ride, and maybe, just maybe, get a ridiculous souvenir photo to commemorate the adventure.

Before We Bid Adieu...

Trauma may have given you PTSD, but it also gave you unmatched strength and a potential membership in the "We Survived and Thrived" club. As we coast into our next chapter, hold on tight; it promises to be a relaxing soak… or at least a deep dive into the world of self-care. Bring your rubber duckies, folks!

Chapter 3

· · · · · · · · · · · · · · · · · · ·

Self–Care: When Spa Days Meet Existential Dread

Ah, "self-care." A term that's blown up faster than a balloon at a kids' party and carries about as many definitions as there are shades of lipstick. With celebs posting their 25-step skincare routine and influencers hailing the next moon-water-retreat (seriously, is that a thing now?), one might think you'd need a PhD to figure it all out. But relax! No PhD required here, just a bit of common sense and maybe a dash of sarcasm.

What Even is Self-Care?

Is it slapping on a face mask while screaming into the void? Is it climbing Mount Everest to "find yourself"? At its core, self-care is just about... well, taking care of yourself. Mind-blowing, right? It's not just treating yourself to that extra scoop of ice cream but ensuring you're mentally, emotionally, and physically okay (or at least aiming for okay-Ish).

Unpacking Trauma's Baggage: "Do I Need a Receipt for This?"

Dealing with trauma's aftermath is like trying to assemble IKEA furniture without the manual. Every screw seems to belong somewhere else, and suddenly you have too many parts. Sure, you wanted a cozy space to relax, but now you're unsure if you've made a coffee table or a portal to another dimension.

- **Routine Building:** Think of it like training for the "Adulting Olympics." The events? Making your bed, not burning toast, and wearing matching socks. Medals are awarded in the form of peaceful mornings and occasional bouts of self-pride.

- **Mental Check-ins:** It's a bit like having a daily chat with your inner computer. You're checking if the emotional software needs updates, clearing cache memories that slow you down, and running a quick scan to keep those pesky anxiety viruses at bay.

- **Physical Care:** Whether you're dancing out your feelings or attempting a single push-up before deciding it's overrated, it's all about movement. Maybe strive for that "two-step" – one step towards the fridge for a snack and another back to the couch. That counts, right?

- **Celebrating Tiny Triumphs:** Managed to wear a shirt that isn't inside out? That's a win! Put on pants today? Give yourself a round of applause. Remember, in the post-trauma game show of life, every little task you nail deserves its moment in the spotlight.

Through all the confusion and challenges, just remember: you're doing the best you can, and that's pretty darn commendable. And if you ever feel lost? Just remember the golden rule of IKEA furniture assembly: when in doubt, take a break and eat some Swedish meatballs.

Elevating Your Self-Care Playbook: From Novice to Ninja

Self-care isn't just about bubble baths and scented candles (although, who can resist lavender's call?). It's about stepping up your game and adding a pinch of pizzazz to the mundane:

- **Therapeutic Activities:** Fancy a dramatic reading of your grocery list? Or how about composing haikus about lost socks? Delve into artsy endeavors that are just as therapeutic as they are entertaining. Your pet might be confused by your interpretive dance about traffic lights, but hey, it's for your soul.

- **Boundaries Bootcamp:** Think of your boundaries as your personal VIP club's velvet rope. Not everyone's on the list. Learn to utter magic phrases like "Not today," "I'll think about it," or the very persuasive, "Only if there's cake involved."

- **Digital Detox Days:** A day off from screens can be liberating! Discover the joys of staring blankly at walls, or indulge in the forgotten art of daydreaming. Ahh, memories of pre-smartphone days where the biggest tech stress was untangling your Walkman's earphones.

- **Trendy Timeouts:** **Ever tried bird-watching in your backyard or apartment window? Or taking a whack** at shadow puppetry during that evening power outage? Sometimes the quirkiest breaks can be the most rejuvenating.

- **Tasty Treat Therapy:** Remember, a little treat doesn't hurt. Whether it's making cloud shapes out of your whipped cream or devouring that bizarrely named exotic fruit just because, find your slice of joy.

So, as you level up in this game called Self-Care, remember it's not about perfection, but enjoying the quirky quests and challenges. Achievement unlocked: Master of Joyful Jibber-Jabber!

Walking the Wobbly Wire: Juggling Life's Challenges

Finding balance in life can feel like you're an untrained circus performer, suddenly thrust into the spotlight with a unicycle, a flaming baton, and a particularly uncooperative poodle to manage. Who signed up for this circus act, anyway?

- **Stiletto Skills Not Required:** Let's be clear; you don't need to strut on your life's tightrope in high heels (or clown shoes, for that matter). It's okay to take it slow, in comfortable footwear, maybe even bunny slippers.

- **Winds of Whimsy:** Just when you think you've got your balance, life likes to blow a gust of wind (or release a flock of pigeons). These unexpected flutters might ruffle your feathers, but remember, everyone looks cool with wind-blown hair.

- **Safety Nets and Bouncy Castles:** While it's important to master your tightrope walk, it's equally vital to ensure there's something soft to land on. Whether it's a safety net, a pile of marshmallows, or a supportive friend named Chris.

- **Audience Applause and Awkward Moments:** As you wobble and waver, you'll have moments of grace and others of...well, less grace. But whether the crowd gasps or claps, it's all part of the show. Plus, any missteps just add to the dramatic tension. Talk about a performance!

- **The Balancing Act Buddy:** Sometimes, it's easier with a friend, especially one with better balance. Join hands, share the load, and make that tightrope walk a duet. Dancing is encouraged, but optional.

Just remember life's balancing act might not come with glitzy costumes or catchy circus tunes, but it's your unique performance. So, step out with confidence, humor, and perhaps a safety helmet (just in case). And remember, the goal isn't to perfect the performance but to enjoy the circus!

There's No "I" in Self-Care... Wait, There Is!

So, you thought self-care was all about solo spa days, journaling your deepest thoughts, and whispering sweet affirmations to yourself in the mirror? Think again! While there's a big fat "I" in self-care, there's also room for a "we", a "you", and even that friend who can't keep a plant alive.

- **Group Masking Sessions:** Picture this: a room full of people with face masks, making them look like a gathering of colorful zombies. You're not just cleansing pores, but also building bonds. Plus, there's the shared hilarity when someone's mask makes them look like Shrek's distant cousin.

- **The Meditation Guessing Game:** As you sit in lotus position, eyes closed, in shared silence, ever wonder what others are thinking? Is Bob pondering the mysteries of the universe, or just hoping he remembered to turn off his latest Netflix binge?

- **Synchronized Stress-Baking:** Ever tried baking with friends? It's chaotic, messy, and there's a high chance someone will be covered in flour. But hey, shared laughter, potential food fights, and at the end, hopefully something edible!

- **"Yoga" With A Twist:** Organize a group yoga session, and watch as everyone pretends to know the difference between "Downward Dog" and "Confused Chameleon." And let's not even get started on who mistakenly thought "Child's Pose" was just lying down and throwing a tantrum.

- **Walking Club (With Optional Gossip):** It's about getting those steps in, breathing in fresh air, and maybe getting the latest scoop on who did what at the last neighborhood gathering. Remember, it's not gossip if you're walking off the calories while doing it!

While self-care is essential and can be deeply personal, there's no rule that says you can't turn it into a party. After all, laughter, shared memories, and that one friend's disastrously funny attempt at a DIY facial can be just as therapeutic as a quiet moment alone. So, grab your pals and make self-care a group extravaganza! Who knew taking care of oneself could be such a riot?

Tying the Bow on the Bumpy Ride of Self-Care Shenanigans

Look, self-care isn't a straight path. Sometimes it feels like riding a rollercoaster while juggling flaming torches and singing the alphabet backward. One day, a serene bubble bath does the trick; the next, you're desperately channeling your inner Shakira with hip gyrations in the living room, hoping the neighbors aren't judging too hard.

The essence of self-care is kind of like a mixtape (remember those?). One day you've got calming Kenny G vibes, and then BAM, you're headbanging to Metallica. And that's the beauty of it! Our needs vary, often ricocheting between "serene spa day" and "let's color everything with neon markers and pretend we're Jackson Pollock."

As you march (or tango, or moonwalk) on this self-care journey, remember that there's no one-size-fits-all. Your personalized care routine might involve chanting affirmations, attending salsa classes, or perhaps mastering the ancient art of not burning popcorn. And on those peculiar days, when only interpretive dances about your feelings for coffee will suffice, go for it! No judgment here.

So as we close this lively chapter on self-care and its many (mis) adventures, let's prepare to embark on our next escapade – therapy! Ah, the magical realm where you spill your wildest dreams and fears, and the person across from you doesn't suggest joining a circus. Stay strapped in, because we're about to dive deep and maybe find a few chuckles along the way. Onward to the therapist's couch – fluffy pillows and all!

Chapter 4

Therapy: The Couch Olympics – Mental Gymnastics and Emotional Hurdles

Ever felt like life is an unsolvable puzzle? Like trying to assemble IKEA furniture with instructions written in hieroglyphics. Enter therapy: the Allen wrench of the soul! A place where you pay someone to listen to you talk, because let's be real, your cat's giving you that judgmental look again.

From Big Screens to Real Scenes: Therapy's Hollywood Makeover

If you think therapy is sitting in a dimly lit room discussing dreams about being chased by giant marshmallows while your therapist nods sagely, think again. Spoiler: It's less about deciphering your dream's marshmallow symbolism and more about why you might be craving s'mores in real life.

Dive Into the Therapy Flavor Fiesta!

Picking a therapy type is like choosing an ice cream flavor when you have a sweet tooth for self-improvement:

- **DBT (Dialectical Behavior Therapy):** Helping you embrace your inner contradictions without turning into a human pretzel.

- **Narrative Therapy:** Reframing your life story to sound less like a tragic opera and more like a quirky indie film.

- **Music Therapy:** A space where belting out 'Bohemian Rhapsody' might just lead to a therapeutic breakthrough.

- **CBT-Therapy:** It's the Marie Kondo for your mind: tidying up thoughts and making space for ones that "spark joy" (and less clutter!).

How Effective is Talking About My Feelings, Really?

Does baring your soul on a comfy couch work? Well, does dancing in your PJs boost your mood? Mostly, yes! But while therapy might not give you that movie montage moment, it promises gradual enlightenment and probably fewer embarrassing dance moves.

- **From Zero to Hero:** Remember those movie moments where a nerdy protagonist gets a snazzy makeover and suddenly everything's rainbows and sunshine? Well, therapy isn't exactly like that. There won't be a background score or dramatic slow-motion, but there will be transformation. Maybe not overnight, but you'll soon be rocking the emotional equivalent of snazzy new glasses and killer confidence.

- **The Not-so-Instant Noodles Approach:** Therapy isn't "just add water" instant. It's a slow simmer, blending the spices of insight, experiences, and professional guidance. The result? A rich broth of understanding that instant noodles could never match. (Sorry, ramen!)

- **Dance Breaks Included:** While therapists might not break into a spontaneous jig with you (though, how fun would that be?), discussing your feelings can be as freeing as those wild, no-one's-watching dance sessions. Fewer jazz hands, more a-ha moments.

- **Couch vs. Karaoke:** While the therapist's couch might not have the thrill of a stage or a flashy mic, it's got its perks. Less stage fright, more insight. Fewer off-key notes, more attuned understanding. And no, you're not getting judged for your song (or life) choices!

- **No More Bottling It Up**: Ever tried shaking a soda bottle and then opening it? Therapy's like gently releasing that cap to let the fizz out, rather than letting it explode in a sticky mess. Only in this analogy, the "fizz" is your bottled-up emotions, and the "sticky mess" is... well, you get the picture.

Ballin' on a Budget: Fancy Therapy Without the Fancy Price Tag

Ever glanced at some therapy price tags and thought, "Is the couch made of gold?" or "Is the therapist going to reveal the meaning of life?". Relax! You don't need to start crowdfunding or consider that underground poker career. There are economical ways to get quality noggin-nurturing:

- **The Wonders of Sliding Scales:** It's like the 'choose your own adventure' of therapy pricing! Some therapists offer a range based on what you can afford, without the side-eye.

- **Intern Therapists:** Think of them as the off-brand cereal of the therapy world. They might not come in the fancy packaging, but they're just as delightful and sometimes, even better. They're up-to-date with the latest techniques and eager to help, all while being supervised by experienced professionals.

- **Community Centers:** The unsung heroes of affordable mental healthcare. These are like those secret menu items at your favorite restaurant - fabulous, effective, and won't make your wallet weep.

- **Group Therapy:** Splitting the bill always sounds good, right? Group sessions can be a way to share costs *and* stories. Plus, who knows, you might find your emotional twin!

- **Online Platforms:** In this digital age, there's an app for almost everything—including therapy! Platforms offer reduced rates and you get to have sessions in your PJs. Win-win!

Remember, mental well-being shouldn't have the price tag of a luxury yacht. With a little savvy searching and a dash of persistence, you can get the support you need without needing to check the couch cushions for spare change. Cheers to emotional enlightenment on a shoestring budget!

Therapists: The Wizards Behind the Curtain

They may be adept at navigating the mind's maze, but remember, therapists are humans too! Maybe they karaoke to 90s pop hits or perhaps they're mastering the art of making the perfect sourdough. They've just got a bit more insight into why you're still mad about that stolen pencil in 3rd grade.

Wrapping Up: Therapy as Your Emotional Workout Regimen

Jumping into therapy is akin to an emotional gym session. Sometimes it's a gentle warm-up, sometimes it's high-intensity interval crying. But the endorphin rush, the clarity, and the emotional six-pack (okay, maybe just a two-pack) make it oh-so-worth it. Up next, we venture into the journey of rediscovery. Because trauma can change you, but it also offers a unique chance to redefine who you are and who you want to be. Stay tuned for the existential fun!

Chapter 5

· · · · · · · · · · · · · · · · · ·

Rediscovering Yourself: From Trauma's Twilight Zone to "Whoa, Did I Just Do That?"

I magine post-trauma life as waking up in an alternate reality where socks have become currency and everyone suddenly speaks fluent Pig Latin. Huh? Exactly. Now you're not just re-learning the ropes; you're also trying to figure out why the ropes are now made of spaghetti. Confusing? Absolutely. An opportunity for growth (and some great stories)? You bet.

The Existential Echo Chamber: "Mirror, Who's This Stranger Staring Back?"

You used to know that face. Now, it looks like it's harboring secrets, like where the missing sock goes in the laundry or why kids love the taste of Cinnamon Toast Crunch. The post-trauma you is a remix, with the same core melody but a new funky beat. Your identity is this intricate quilt of experiences, interests, and that one embarrassing memory from high school. Trauma might add a few unexpected patches, but hey, maybe neon polka dots next to vintage paisley is a trend waiting to happen.

The Twists, Turns, and Tuba Lessons of Post-Trauma Interests

Alright, let's address the unicorn in the room. Post-trauma, our brain occasionally goes on a wild shopping spree in the hobby store of life. One moment you're all about that mindful meditation, and the next, you're considering competitive unicorn racing. (Side note: If you find out where this is happening, please send directions.)

- **Extreme Origami:** Suddenly, you're up at 3 AM, trying to fold a paper replica of the Eiffel Tower. Will it stand? Probably not. But hey, at least now you have a crumpled monument of dedication!

- **The Lure of the Didgeridoo:** That deep, resonating sound that most people can't identify? You're determined to master it. Your neighbors might start wearing earplugs, but when you nail "Twinkle Twinkle Little Star" on that bad boy, it'll be worth it.

- **Knitting, But With Flair:** Why make a scarf when you can knit a full-scale model of the solar system? (Saturn's rings are trickier than they look.)

- **Unicorn Racing:** It might sound mythical, but the thrill of racing atop a unicorn (or a very well-disguised horse) can be oddly therapeutic. Just remember to hold onto the mane and watch out for the occasional rainbow roadblock.

- **Synchronized Spatula Dancing:** Combining the art of dance with... kitchen utensils? It might not make it to the Olympics, but your breakfast pancakes will have never seen such flair.

- **Learning Elvish:** Because sometimes, connecting with fictional characters feels more grounding than that high school reunion you've been avoiding.

The Great Basket-Weaving Fiasco: It's All Part of the Plan!

Listen, not every skill or hobby is going to be your golden ticket to relaxation and self-enlightenment. So, you gave basket weaving a whirl, and instead of a basket, you ended up with... a modern art masterpiece? Or perhaps a nest for a really confused bird? Bravo!

Remember, it's like dating. Not every match is "the one." Sometimes you're set up with a hobby that, on paper, seems like a dream. But in practice? It's more of a second-cousin-twice-removed kind of vibe. And hey, that's okay!

The goal is to find what resonates with you. And if the rhythmic dance of basket weaving made you more frantic than a cat in a bathtub, then it's just not your groove. Don't sweat it. On the plus side, you've now got an epic story to share at parties, "Did I ever tell you about the time I tried basket weaving?"

The point is, life's too short to force a coping skill that feels as awkward as wearing socks with sandals. If one strategy doesn't mesh with you, toss it in your "tried that" bin and move onto the next. Before you know it, you'll have an arsenal of go-to's (and a few hilarious not-for-me's) that help you navigate the choppy waters of life.

In conclusion, today's "basket breakdown" might just be tomorrow's comedic gold. So, keep exploring, keep laughing at the missteps, and most importantly, keep weaving your unique tapestry of life (even if it doesn't include actual weaving).

Relationships: The Good, The Bad, and the "Why Are We Discussing Alpaca Farming?"

Ah, the ever-evolving tapestry of post-trauma relationships. It's a blend of nostalgia, bewilderment, and the occasional furry creature:

- **Strengthened Bonds:** There are those relationships that prove to be as hardy as that Nokia 3310 you owned back in the day. Remember when it fell down two flights of stairs, took a brief swim in your coffee, and still managed to have three bars of battery left by the end of the week? That's this relationship. Resilient, timeless, and with a knack for the game of Snake.

- **Sudden Detours:** Then there are the connections that take sudden, alpaca-sized detours. One day you're discussing weekend plans, the next you're deep into a debate about whether alpacas or llamas give better side-eye. Or pondering starting an alpaca-themed band. Spoiler: Alpacas are the superior side-eye givers, but don't tell the llamas we said that.

- **New Allies:** As you weave through this maze of relationships, you'll also bump into fellow adventurers. These are the folks who don't just humor your newfound interest in alpaca trivia but genuinely ponder if alpacas are part of a cute, fluffy group planning to take over the world. I mean, have you seen those eyes? They're clearly plotting *something*.

In summary, post-trauma relationships are a wild ride, oscillating between the robustness of vintage tech and the unpredictable whimsy of alpaca herding. So as you navigate this terrain, remember to cherish the Snake-playing Nokias in your life, be open to the occasional alpaca detour, and always keep an eye out for potential fluffy overlords. Onward to more shenanigans!

The "No" Jutsu Chronicles: Harnessing Your Inner Emotional Ninja

Welcome, grasshopper, to the sacred dojo of "No" Jutsu, where the ancient art of boundary-setting meets modern-day sass. If trauma has taught you anything, it's that life's too short for wishy-washy maybes. Time to channel that inner ninja!

- **The Swift deflect:** Your newly honed "No" can deflect unsolicited advice like a pro fencer parries a thrust. Aunt Karen suggesting another weird remedy for your woes? Deflected!

- **The Ninja Vanish:** When situations or conversations get too heavy, "No" Jutsu teaches you the subtle art of the ninja vanish. It's the elegant exit, without the smoke bomb, though feel free to use one for added drama.

- **The Emotional Block:** Picture this: a barrage of unwanted invitations, guilt trips, and awkward conversations come flying at you. But with your "No" Jutsu training, you're able to block them with the grace of a cat sidestepping an overenthusiastic toddler.

- **Summoning the Support Scrolls:** True ninjas know the power of allies. So, when your "No" needs an extra oomph, summon your support scrolls – be it friends, self-help books, or that barista who just gets it.

- **The Sacred Self-Care Seal:** This powerful move is the ultimate culmination of your "No" Jutsu training. It's the act of prioritizing yourself, sealing off from energy drainers, and channeling all that good chakra towards self-renewal.

Remember, young ninja, "No" Jutsu isn't about becoming an impenetrable fortress but rather cultivating a sanctuary. It's about asserting your space in the world, with a gentle (or not-so-gentle) reminder that you've got the reflexes and the moves to keep your emotional dojo serene. So, keep practicing, keep parrying, and maybe, just maybe, throw in a somersault for style points!

Celebrating Mundanity: Because Toast Can be Triumph

In a world where achievements are usually measured in grand gestures and viral moments, let's take a moment to salute the unsung heroes of daily life: the mundane triumphs. Because let's face it, in the epic saga of post-trauma recovery, sometimes the real dragon to be slain is that daunting laundry pile.

- **The Perfect Pour:** Managed to pour your cereal without spilling half of it on the counter? That's not just breakfast; that's performance art.

- **Mismatched Socks? Fashion Statement!:** Who said your socks need to match? Today, you managed to find two. Period. And that, my friend, screams avant-garde fashion.

- **Elevator Etiquette Mastery:** Successfully avoided that awkward small talk with a neighbor by pretending to be engrossed in your phone? Oscar-worthy acting right there!

- **Plant Parenthood:** So, your plant has drooped a bit. But it's still green(ish), and it's still alive! You're not just a plant parent; you're fostering plant resilience!

- **The TV Remote Conquest:** Found the remote on the first try without dismantling your entire living room? Sounds like a Sherlock-level deduction to me.

- **Microwave DJ:** Nailed the exact timing on the microwave so your leftovers were heated evenly? Forget being a cook; you're the DJ of microwave beeps.

- **Shoelace Showdown:** Tied both shoes with equal tightness? That's not just adulting; that's advanced adulting!

At the end of the day, it's these little sprinkles of normalcy, these mini-moments of mastery, that deserve a standing ovation (or at least a comfy seated clap). Because when life's a whirlwind, there's something beautifully rebellious about celebrating the fact that you, yes YOU, nailed that toast without triggering the smoke alarm. So, here's to the mundane, the everyday, and the hilariously ordinary moments that make life's blooper reel so darn worth it!

Dressing Up in Feelings:
The Runway Show of the Soul

If emotions were outfits, some of us would have wardrobes rivaling the grandeur of a celebrity closet. And just like fashion, emotions are ever-changing, sometimes seasonal, and occasionally just downright confusing. Welcome to the chic boutique of feelings, where every day is a fashion show, and the world (well, your living room) is your runway.

- **Teary-eyed Tuesdays:** This is the "vintage" ensemble that sometimes makes a comeback. It's reminiscent of past moments, paired perfectly with tissues and maybe a bar of chocolate. You wear it with a touch of nostalgia and a dab of 'sniffle-chic'.

- **Wonderstruck Wednesdays:** The fabulous flair of feeling amazed by the simplest things, like realizing your socks actually match or discovering a forgotten $5 bill in your jeans. It's the emotional equivalent of stumbling upon a retro jacket that still fits.

- **Therapeutic Thursdays:** Ever tried donning the "Robe of Reflection" or perhaps the "Silk Pajamas of Self-awareness"?

These are the days when introspection becomes your chosen accessory, perhaps paired with a diary or a meditation app.

- **Frazzled Fridays:** This ensemble is a mix of "Weekend Excitement" with undertones of "Did I Forget to Turn Off the Coffee Maker?" It's like wearing high-heels with pajama bottoms – a delightful combo of anticipation and oops-I-forgot.

- **Soulful Sundays:** A day when the mood is calm pastels, the rhythm is slow, and the attire screams "Zen-Zen Baby!" Whether it's draped in gratitude or the soft scarf of solitude, Sundays let you lounge in the easy-chair of emotions.

- **Mix 'n' Match Moments:** Then there are days when emotions feel like every piece of clothing you own thrown onto a bed, and you're just trying to see what sticks. It's the bold fashion choice of "I-have-no-idea-what-I'm-feeling" – and that's okay!

- **Couture of Confidence:** And sometimes, just sometimes, amidst the varied outfits and dramatic drapes, you find that evergreen classic – the Little Black Dress of Confidence or the Snazzy Suit of Self-belief.

In the grand dressing room of life, remember that it's okay to have wardrobe malfunctions and days when you're just draped in duvet covers of doubt. Embrace every style, strut your stuff, and know that you're absolutely rocking the runway of emotions. After all, what's life without a little (or a lot) of emotional flair?

In Conclusion: Rocking the Rollercoaster

The rediscovery ride post-trauma isn't a straight, breezy road; it's a rollercoaster, with its ups, downs, and loop-de-loops. And while it might make you scream, throw your hands up, or even laugh at the sheer absurdity, remember this: every twist is carving out a more complex, resilient, and vibrant you. Brace yourselves; up next is an exploration into humor's healing hocus pocus. Unravel how a hearty laugh can be the ultimate spell against despair.

Chapter 6

Laughter: The Slapstick Response to Life's Slap-in-the-Face Moments

Life: It's less of a well-scripted Oscar-winning drama and more of a series of bloopers that never made it to the final cut. In this feature film called existence, it's essential to find moments of comic relief between the epic plot twists and intense drama. Prepare your popcorn, because the comedy reel is about to roll.

- **Gravity Checks:** Ever walked confidently into a room only to trip over... well, your own enthusiasm? That's life's way of conducting random gravity checks. Thankfully, floors are great listeners. They'll always be there for you—especially when you fall for them.

- **Mysterious Sock Monster:** It's a universal conundrum. You put two socks in the wash and only one emerges. Where do they go? Is there a sock rave happening in another dimension? It's one of life's laughable mysteries that keeps us chuckling and perplexed.

- **Tech Fails:** Ever been on an important video call when your cat decides to flaunt its derrière to your boss? Or how about those awkward moments when auto-correct changes "Kind Regards" to "King Radish"? Digital blunders remind us that even in the age of AI, the universe has a cheeky sense of humor.

- **The Great Grocery Saga:** You venture to the store for bread. You return with five bags of random stuff... but forget the bread. It's as if our brains play mini games of "Forget the Essential" every time we shop. Makes for a good chuckle and another 'unexpected' trip to the store.

- **Awkward Elevator Encounters:** You enter, press your floor, and then someone else comes in and stands *just* a little too close. Cue the longest 20 seconds of your life, complete with weird humming and an over-analysis of the elevator's carpet pattern. Ah, the joys of shared discomfort!

- **DIY Disasters:** From assembling furniture where you're left with 'extra' parts to trying out a new recipe that looks more like an alien lifeform than food, DIY attempts remind us that it's okay to laugh at our wonderfully human imperfections.

- **Hair-raising Haircuts:** We've all been there. You show the stylist a picture of a Hollywood celeb, hoping for a touch of glam, but you leave looking like their distant second cousin—twice removed. Hair grows back, but the giggles from those "unique" hair days linger forever.

- **Bizarre Dreams Featuring... Llamas?** Sometimes our sub-conscious decides to host a wild party featuring flying llamas or singing potatoes. Waking up from such dreams, all you can do is chuckle and wonder, "Brain, what were you on last night?"

At the end of the day, laughter serves as life's delightful blooper reel. It's those unscripted, off-cue moments that make the journey memorable. So, when life pelts you with pies or plays pranks that leave you puzzled, remember to chuckle, guffaw, or snort. Because in this grand, chaotic production, sometimes you've got to laugh at the outtakes and appreciate the retakes.

Laughter Tunes: Adjusting the Volume and Frequency

Every individual has their own "comedy frequency." For some, it's the subtle sarcasm, while others lean more towards the "dad jokes" spectrum (you know, the ones that are so bad, they're good?). And then there's that special category of people who laugh at puns so much; they can't help but "pun-der" why others don't get it. The trick is finding and fine-tuning your frequency, so you're laughing with life, not feeling laughed at.

The Comedy Buffet: Taste-testing Different Humor Dishes

Venturing into the world of humor is like stepping into an all-you-can-laugh buffet. From dark humor that's a bit like that mys-terious spicy dish (packed with a punch and not for everyone) to light-hearted slapstick that's akin to the comfort food section, sample a bit of everything. Find out if you're more of a "dry wit" appetizer person or if "silly spoofs" are your main course.

Crafting Your "Jest-List": A Comedy Playlist for the Soul

Create a go-to list of comedic content that's bound to lift your spirits on dreary days. This could range from that episode of a sitcom where the character wears pants on their head (we all have *that* day) to stand-up clips that tackle life's ironies with just the right touch. And let's not forget those compilations of cats being... well, cats. Because feline tomfoolery is a universal spirit-lifter!

In Closing: Embrace the Giggles, Mind the Puddles

Finding humor after trauma is a delicate dance, indeed. But with the right tunes and moves, you can waltz, tango, or even moon-walk through life's puddles. Just remember to wear non-slip shoes, or better yet, embrace the occasional splash! After all, life isn't about avoiding the comedic puddles—it's about dancing in the rain with a laugh track in the background. Next up, we're diving deep into the world of post-trauma relationships. Buckle up for an exploration of bonds, barriers, and finding beauty amidst the bruises. Ready for a heart-to-heart journey? Step right this way!

Chapter 7

....

Relationships After Trauma: It's Not You, It's... Actually, Maybe It's Both of Us?

After trauma, managing relationships can feel like trying to assemble IKEA furniture— all the pieces look familiar, but why the heck are there so many leftover screws? Whether it's friends, family, or lovers, let's explore this "assembly required" phase of post-trauma relationships.

The Seismic Shift in Interactions

Post-trauma, social interactions might feel like playing a board game where someone changed all the rules overnight. One day, you're a pro at Monopoly, and the next, it seems everyone else is playing Clue, and you're the only one left clueless.

The Friend Spectrum: From Angels to Anchors

Every trauma survivor quickly realizes there's a broad spectrum of friends:

- **The Rockstars:** Those wonderful souls who, even if they don't fully get it, always have your back, supplying tissues, chocolate, or cheesy 90s songs as needed.

- **The Clueless Counselors:** Their heart's in the right place, but their advice? Not so much. "Have you tried not being traumatized?" Thanks, Brenda. Why didn't I think of that?

Love in the Time of Trauma: The Roller Coaster Ride

Ah, romance post-trauma. If it was a movie genre, it'd be a rom-com-drama-thriller, all in one. A little laughter, a sprinkle of tears, and some unexpected plot twists. Like trying to light a romantic candle and accidentally setting off the fire alarm. You know, the usual.

- **Emotional Detours:** You might find yourself in unexpected territory. One minute, you're planning a romantic dinner, and the next, you're both in the middle of a heated debate about which cereal mascot is the most trustworthy. Hint: It's not Tony the Tiger. He's too grrrrreat to be trusted.

- **Rebuilding Intimacy:** This isn't just about reigniting the flames (hopefully without any fire alarms). It's about navigating the emotional minefield together. Sometimes it's reading the intricate love language of "left the last piece of chocolate for you." Other times, it's communicating in Morse code through blanket forts.

- **Love Quizzes Galore:** Remember those teen magazines with compatibility quizzes? Now's a good time to whip them out. "Is your partner more of a sunset or sunrise?" might sound cheesy, but hey, at least you're both laughing!

- **Couples Therapy:** The GPS of Love: This isn't just for relationships on the rocks. Consider it preventive maintenance. It's like taking your relationship car for a tune-up. Oil change, check the brakes, and ensure both hearts are still in sync. And if you end up in a roundabout of emotions, it's that voice guiding you: "Take the second exit towards understanding."

- **Managing the Speed Bumps:** Trauma can introduce some, let's call them, "interesting" dynamics. Like, who knew pillow forts would become a vital tool in communication? Or that a shared playlist titled "Songs for When Words Fail" would be your go-to?

- **The Power of 'We':** There's something potent in facing challenges as a unit. Even if sometimes it feels like you're two peas in a very, very wonky pod. But remember, peas in pods stick together, no matter how twisty the pod gets.

In the wild ride of love post-trauma, it's not just about holding on tight; it's about enjoying the scenic detours, the unplanned pit stops, and the hilarious, unexpected adventures.

Family Ties: A Mixtape of Love and Misunderstandings

If families were TV shows, they'd be an ever-changing blend of reality TV, sitcom, and those mystery shows where every episode leaves you more confused than the last. Throw in trauma, and suddenly it's a spicy season with cliffhangers and unexpected plot twists.

- **Understanding vs. Undermining:** Aunt Gertrude, with her constant "Back in my day, we didn't have traumas; we just had long walks to school!" Well, bless her heart, but sometimes you wish she'd understand trauma isn't the same as her walks uphill both ways.

- **Cousin Know-it-All:** There's always that one family member with advice on *everything*. "Have you tried yoga? How about essential oils? Or maybe stand on one foot during a full moon?" Thanks, but no thanks, cousin Sally.

- **Setting Limits:** Remember when you tried to set parental controls on the family TV? Think of boundaries as the "adult version" of that. Only this time, you're blocking unsolicited advice and overbearing hugs, not late-night shows.

- **Family Group Chats:** A Double-Edged Sword: On one hand, they're great for updates; on the other hand, you're now privy to Uncle Bob's daily musings on squirrels in his backyard and daily weather reports from grandma.

- **Memory Lane Pitfalls:** Family gatherings can sometimes feel like you're on a "This is Your Life" game show. Flashbacks! Nostalgia! Cringe-worthy memories! Remember that time you wore a turkey on your head at Thanksgiving? They sure do.

- **The Unexpected Allies:** Surprisingly, trauma can reveal unexpected champions in your family. That silent uncle? He might share a profound piece of wisdom. The teenage cousin? They might introduce you to a calming app or a song that resonates.

- **Holiday Hoopla:** The holidays can become a cacophony of questions like "How are you now?" and unsolicited advice. But hey, at least there's pie! And if you need an escape, just say you're on a new "Pie and Silence" meditation regime.

Family, with all its quirks and quibbles, is an intricate tapestry of ties that bind. Through the highs, lows, and "What on earth are they thinking?!" moments, there's comfort in this collective chaos. And if all else fails? There's always pie. Did I mention the pie?

Navigating the Office Jungle: Beyond Coffee Breaks

Your workplace post-trauma isn't just about the 9 to 5 grind; it's more like a safari adventure, minus the picturesque sunsets (unless you've got a killer office view). Here's how to be the Jane or Tarzan of this concrete jungle:

- **Transparent Talks:** HR doesn't exactly serve as the wildlife guide, but think of them as the ranger helping you avoid the metaphorical potholes. They might not regale you with tales of lion prides, but they can offer support options or adjusted duties.

- **Work-life balance:** Balancing work and life isn't about being the tightrope prodigy; it's more akin to a trapeze artist. You swing, you leap, and sometimes, you need a safety net (or a really comfy couch) to land on.

- **Tackling the Email Elephant:** That mounting unread count can feel like an elephant sitting on your motivation. Tame the beast with folders, labels, or by occasionally setting an "I am currently out of the office mentally" auto-response.

- **Meeting Meerkats:** Meetings can pop up unexpectedly, just like curious meerkats. While Bob from accounting's surprise update might not be as adorable, remember: every meeting is one step closer to your lunch break.

- **Avoiding Water Cooler Crocodiles:** Small talk by the cooler can sometimes veer into murky waters, especially with nosy colleagues. Equip yourself with breezy, non-committal answers and master the art of the swift escape. "Oh look, my plant needs watering!"

- **Desk Decor - Your Emotional Oasis:** Turn your workspace into a serene oasis amidst the chaos. Be it stress-relieving squishy toys, calming plants (yes, even if it's a cactus named Spike), or motivational sticky notes reminding you that "You've got this!"

- **Lunch Breaks - Your Safari Retreat:** Make lunch breaks your mini retreat. If the office cafeteria feels like a lion's den, maybe find a peaceful perch in a nearby park. Or if your colleagues sound more like hyenas, pop in those headphones and drift away.

In the vast savannah of the corporate world, remember: while there are challenges aplenty, there are also oases of calm, allies in unexpected corners, and yes, always the thrill of the wild (or at least the office Christmas party). Swing on, Tarzan! Swing on!

Drawing Lines in the Sand: Boundaries 101

Navigating post-trauma emotions? Think of it as directing traffic in the bustling city of "You-topia." Everyone wants to zip through, but without some solid road rules, it's going to be a honk-filled mess. So, here's how to lay down those lanes:

- **The Emotional Toll Booth:** Not everyone gets free access. Some folks need to earn their way, maybe by showing understanding, patience, or just by having really good snacks.

- **Roundabouts of Reassurance:** These are your safe zones. When things get overwhelming, take a few loops here. It's where you remind yourself that it's okay to take things slow and to reroute if needed.

- **Speed Bumps and Slow Zones:** Some topics or people might require more delicate handling. These are the areas in your life where you need to slow down, take a deep breath, and proceed with caution. And if someone's rushing you? Flash them your "Chill, I'm taking my time" signal.

- **VIP Lanes:** Reserved for those who've proven they can cruise alongside you without causing a 10-car pile-up of emotions. These are the folks who get your journey, no map needed.

- **Parking Zones:** Sometimes, you need to park, reflect, and just sit with your feelings. Find your designated spots— be it a cozy corner in your home, a favorite park, or a cafe where the barista (miraculously) gets your name right every time.

- **The No-Entry Zones:** There are alleys and lanes that are strictly off-limits. It could be topics you're not ready to delve into or people whose energy feels more like a demolition derby. It's okay to put up a "Do Not Enter" sign, no explanations needed.

- **Emergency Exits:** Always have a few escape routes planned. These are your quick getaways for when a conversation turns tricky or a situation becomes too sticky. It could be a change of topic, a handy distraction, or just the age-old "Look over there!" trick.

- **The Honk-Happy Drivers:** Let's face it, some folks are just eager to honk, rush, and zoom without regard for the rules. Your task? Stay calm, signal your intent, and remember: Your road, your rules.

As you cruise through the avenues and boulevards of post-trauma life, remember to enjoy the scenery, blast your favorite tunes, and always wear your seatbelt. After all, every road trip (literal or emotional) is about the journey, not just the destination. Safe driving!

Building Your Post-Trauma Tribe

As you begin the quest to assemble your post-trauma tribe, it's less about sending out a beacon into the night sky and more about recognizing those hidden heroes around you. So, let's roll out the tribe recruitment drive:

- Captain Empathy: They may not have a shield, but their superpower is understanding. They're the ones who nod knowingly, offering a comforting pat when your story sounds more like a soap opera plot than real life.

- Doctor Listener: With the patience of a saint and the keen ear of a top-notch detective, this tribal member hears between the lines. They'll pick up on that sigh, that unsaid word, making you feel truly heard. No magic cape needed.

- The Iron(wo)man of Resourcefulness: Not built in a high-tech cave but someone with an uncanny knack for finding solutions. Need a recommendation for a budget-friendly therapist or a recipe for gluten-free brownies? They're on it!

- Hulk Hugger: Their hugs are transformational. Having a bad day? One embrace from them, and it's like being wrapped in a warm duvet of understanding. They might not smash, but they sure envelop!

- Black Widow of Boundaries: This tribe member teaches you the sacred art of saying "No". They're an expert at weaving protective webs, ensuring no emotional vampires suck the life out of you.

- Thor, God of Encouragement: With a booming voice (and hopefully less Shakespearean dialogue), they're your biggest cheerleader, always ready with a pep talk and maybe a mythical hammer to smash through obstacles.

- Guardians of the Group Chats: They're the unsung heroes. The ones who send uplifting memes at 3 AM, start a spontaneous dance challenge, or simply check in with a "How you doin'?".

- Ant-person of Perspective: They might seem small or soft-spoken, but their ability to offer a fresh viewpoint? Monumental! They show you the big picture when you're stuck staring at a pixel.

- Captain Marvelous Motivator: Bursting in with cosmic energy, they're the ones who'll drag you to that new yoga class or join you in that weirdly enticing pottery workshop.

- Nick or Nicole Fury, the Organizer: Every tribe needs its orchestrator, someone with an eye (or eyepatch) on the bigger picture, rallying the group when spirits wane.

Building your tribe isn't about finding superheroes, but recognizing the super within ordinary folks. It's an ensemble cast, each member contributing their own brand of quirky magic. So, as you build your tribe, remember: You might not be fighting intergalactic villains, but you're battling, healing, and growing together. And that's what makes this team-up truly marvelous!

Wrapping Up: Relationships Are Like Puzzles

Navigating post-trauma relationships is like doing a jigsaw puzzle where the pieces keep changing shapes. But with patience, understanding, and a dollop of humor, the picture starts to come together, creating a beautiful tapestry of connections. Next on our journey, we tackle the world of future aspirations post-trauma. How do dreams evolve, and how can you chase them with a renewed sense of purpose? Tie those shoelaces; it's going to be an inspiring sprint!

Chapter 8

. . . .

Future Plans: Because "Winging It" Needs an Upgrade

Post-trauma, plotting your path forward might feel like trying to program a VCR in the 90s - blinking, confusing, and every now and then you accidentally reset everything. Yet, amid the glitches and befuddlements, there's room for planning, ambition, and yes, some side-splitting slip-ups.

The GPS of Life: Recalculating Route...

Remember those old-school car GPS devices that kept saying "recalculating" every time you made a wrong turn? Post-trauma life can feel like that, but instead of a monotone voice, it's your inner critic wondering why you took the metaphorical left at a roundabout.

- **The Unexpected Detours:** Just when you think you're on the highway to Healingville, your GPS might send you down an alley named "Random Crying Spurt Lane." Don't fret; this alley has the best emotional taco stand.

- **Roadblocks and Emotional Potholes:** Navigating around past traumas can feel like avoiding potholes on a rainy day. Sometimes you'll swerve; sometimes, you'll hit one and spill your emotional coffee. Remember, everyone has their bumpy stretches.

- **Sudden U-Turns:** Remember that thing you said you'd never do? Like adopting seven cats or learning the ukulele? Surprise! Your GPS just recalculated, and now you're on a path sprinkled with catnip and strumming "Somewhere Over the Rainbow."

- **Overenthusiastic Voice Prompts:** Your internal GPS voice isn't always the calm, collected type. Sometimes it sounds like an overexcited game show host. "In 5 seconds, make a DECISION! Right or left? Pick now! Oh, and here's a flashback from third grade!"

- **The Occasional No-Signal Zone:** Just like in those remote countryside drives, there might be moments when you feel you've lost the signal, aimlessly drifting. But soon enough, after some introspective static, the signal (and direction) usually returns.

- **The Scenic Route:** Sometimes the best discoveries come when you're not on the fastest route. The winding trails, those moments of introspection, or the random detours into "What-am-I-doing?" Valley often have the best views and lessons.

- **Constant Updates:** Just like apps, your inner GPS will have regular updates. New versions might come with fresh insights, refined directions, or even funky new ringtones (like the tune of "I've got this!")

- **Battery Saving Mode:** Occasionally, you might need to go offline, save some energy, and recalibrate. Rest stops are essential. Recharge, refuel, and then rev up for the next leg of the journey.

Life post-trauma isn't about reaching a set destination via the most direct route. It's about the journey, the detours, the scenic overlooks, and yes, even those pesky "recalculating" moments. Keep your eyes on the road, your hands upon the wheel, and maybe consider upgrading to the latest GPS model every once in a while!

The Roundabout of Emotional Redirects: "Wait, Was That My Exit?"

Life post-trauma isn't a straightforward highway; it's more like a road with more roundabouts than a British town center. And with these circular challenges come the unexpected detours:

- The Surprise U-Turns: Just when you think you've mastered the map, life throws in a U-turn. Maybe it's a sudden urge to learn the art of interpretive salsa dancing or a newfound passion for collecting spoons. Embrace it. After all, who knew the back of spoons could be so fascinating?

- "Was That My Exit?" Moments: Sometimes, you might miss the obvious turns. Like forgetting why you walked into a room or accidentally signing up for an underwater basket-weaving class when you meant yoga. But hey, underwater baskets could be the next big thing!

- Pit Stops for Soul Snacks: Not every stop needs to be planned. Sometimes, you just need to pull over, marvel at the world's largest rubber band ball (or your emotional equivalent), and grab a treat. Emotional snack bars, anyone?

- Navigating Roundabouts of Reflection: You might find yourself going in circles (mentally), revisiting feelings or memories. But with every loop, you gain clarity, understanding, and perhaps a funny anecdote about that one time you circled a roundabout five times because you couldn't decide on an exit.

- Backup Routes with Quirky Landmarks: The main road might be blocked with a parade of past memories, so why not take that side route? Sure, it's dotted with bizarre landmarks like the "Museum of Failed DIY Projects" or "Cafe of Regrettable Haircuts," but they add color to the journey.

- The Surprise Shortcut: Just when you're bracing for a long detour, you stumble upon a shortcut. Maybe it's a newfound coping mechanism or a hilarious podcast that feels like therapy. Score!

- Travel Companions & Hitchhikers: Along the way, you might pick up fellow travelers. Some are there for the long haul, others just for a brief yet memorable karaoke session. Either way, they add tunes to your journey.

In essence, navigating the unexpected U-turns and detours of life isn't about reaching the destination swiftly. It's about enjoying the journey, taking in the sights, singing loudly to car karaoke, and maybe, just maybe, finding the best ice cream cone along the way. Safe travels and don't forget to rate your trip!

Life Dreams 2.0: The "Plot Twist" Edition

So, life threw a wrench in your master plan and, post-trauma, your goals went from being a neatly stacked Jenga tower to a scattered game of 52-card pickup. But guess what? It's revamp time! Welcome to the shiny, somewhat chaotic, yet ever-entertaining version of your aspirations.

- **The New Top 10 List:** Pre-trauma, maybe it was about climbing the corporate ladder. Now? It's mastering the art of climbing into bed by 9 PM and conquering the world of dreamland. Both have their merits (and dragons to slay).

- **Bucket List Bingo:** Your new bucket list might have swapped out "Swim with Sharks" for "Successfully Avoid Spoilers of My Favorite Show." Equally adrenaline-pumping, especially in a world dominated by social media.

- **Travel Goals - Couch Edition:** Instead of globetrotting, you're now show-hopping – visiting different countries and time periods, all from the comfort of your couch. Tardis or Netflix? Who can tell the difference?

- **Financial Planning... For Ice Cream:** Investment portfolios are crucial, but have you considered diversifying your ice cream flavors? A cone in hand beats two in the freezer. Risky? Maybe. Rewarding? Absolutely!

- **Hobbies Reimagined:** Before, it was about marathon running. Now, it's the marathon watching of a series. And let's face it, binging a show without bathroom breaks is an endurance sport.

- **Dress Code:** PJs All Day! If fashion runways started showcasing pajamas, you'd be miles ahead. Comfort is the new couture, and fuzzy socks are the ultimate accessory.

- **Culinary Dreams:** Perhaps before you dreamt of dining at a five-star restaurant. Now, it's about nailing that five-ingredient recipe without setting off the smoke alarm. Both offer a sense of accomplishment and an aroma... of sorts.

- **Pet Priorities:** Owning a ranch with horses sounds fancy, but have you considered the joy of a single, derpy goldfish that might just think you're god?

- **Language Goals:** Learning French or Italian might've been the plan, but now, understanding the lingo of youngsters is the challenge. "Yeet" isn't a form of greeting, apparently.

- **Zen Zone:** Meditation retreats in Tibet sound idyllic, but attaining zen while navigating a supermarket sale? Now that's enlightenment in action!

- **The Timeline Tango:** Forget societal timelines, benchmarks, and the constant ticking of life's metaphorical clock. It's time to do the Timeline Tango, where you move at your rhythm, make your music, and decide when and how to take the next step.

In short, the post-trauma shuffle is less about downgrading dreams and more about remixing them. It's a vibrant mashup of old desires, new priorities, and a generous sprinkle of quirky aspirations. And remember, life isn't a straight path, it's more like a cha-cha. Step back, step forward, and add a little twirl!

In Summation: The Dance of Determination and Delight

While trauma might have momentarily stalled your groove, the music's far from over. With each step, slide, shuffle, and occasional stumble, you're choreographing a dance that's uniquely yours. It's a blend of determination, resilience, and those delightful moments of spontaneous hilarity. Next up, we're delving deep into the world of unexpected molehills (and mountains) life keeps tossing our way. Ever felt like just as you've whacked one challenge down, two more pop up in its place? Get ready to master the art of agility, resilience, and maybe even improve your high score along the way. Onward to the arcade of life!

Chapter 9

....

Embracing the Unexpected: Life's Wild Game of Whack-a-Mole.

Ever played Whack-a-Mole? One moment everything's calm, and the next, little critters are popping up left, right, and center. Well, imagine the moles are life's unpredictability, and the mallet is... well, still a mallet, but metaphorically speaking. Trauma can make life feel like an advanced level of this game, but with more plot twists and fewer tickets for prizes.

"Plot Twist!" – Your New Catchphrase

Just when you think you've got the hang of things, life yells, "Plot twist!" and suddenly you're trying to learn the ukulele or figuring out why avocados are a superfood. Embrace these bizarre turns and remember: every plot twist adds depth to your story (and sometimes a chuckle or two).

The Emotional Rollercoaster: No Height Requirements

On this wild ride of life post-trauma, there are ups, downs, and those loop-de-loops that leave you questioning your lunch choices. While it might be tempting to hop off, remember: the view from the peaks is breathtaking, and the valleys? They make the highs even more worthwhile.

Befriending Murphy and His Law

Anything that can go wrong will go wrong. Or so says Murphy's Law. But here's a secret: Murphy can be a fun guy! Embracing the unexpected means occasionally laughing at the absurdity, even if it's just a chuckle about spilled milk turning into an impromptu kitchen slip 'n slide.

Your Life Soundtrack: Now Featuring More Cowbell!

Every epic journey needs a soundtrack. While yours might have its share of melancholic ballads, don't forget to add some cowbell solos. Why? Because cowbells are ridiculous, and sometimes you need a reminder to not take everything so seriously.

The Twists in the Plot: Not Just for Soap Operas

Life might start feeling a tad soap opera-ish with all its drama and unexpected events. Alien abductions aside, these twists keep things... well, interesting. Plus, they give you ample material for that memoir you've been pondering.

"Who Ordered This?!" Embracing Unwanted Deliveries

Imagine life as a restaurant where you sometimes get dishes you never ordered. While trauma might feel like getting served pickled octopus instead of apple pie, it's an opportunity to develop a taste for the unfamiliar. Or, at the very least, a funny story at parties.

That Sudden Interest in Alpaca Farming

Trauma can manifest in strange ways, including sudden and inexplicable interests. If you find yourself deep-diving into the world of alpaca farming at 3 AM, just roll with it. Who knows? It might be therapeutic. Plus, alpacas are pretty darn cute.

Wrapping Up: The Game Show Continues

As you juggle life's curveballs, remember it's okay to drop a ball or two (or seven). The goal isn't perfection; it's persistence. And a good laugh, even if it's at the sheer wackiness of it all. As the curtains draw on this chapter, get ready to embark on our final act where we take a bow or do the robot dance!

Chapter 10

....

The Encore: Trauma's Afterparty

Imagine surviving the emotional rollercoaster of trauma, only to find yourself at its afterparty. The music is a mix of somber ballads and peppy pop, the dress code is "wear your emotions," and the snacks? Well, they range from bittersweet chocolate to spicy revelations. Welcome to the encore of our journey.

The Uninvited Guests: Lingering Emotions

Just like any party, there are bound to be a few crashers. Anger, guilt, or sadness might waltz in unannounced. But instead of throwing them out, perhaps give them a moment. Dance a dance, share a laugh, and then gently guide them to the exit when you're ready.

Karaoke Corner: Finding Your Voice

At this afterparty, there's a karaoke machine where you can belt out your truths. Whether it's a soulful ballad about your struggles or a rocking anthem of resilience, grab that mic. Even if you're tone-deaf, it's about catharsis, not concert-quality!

Mood Lighting: The Highs and Lows

The ambiance at this shindig varies. Some corners are illuminated by the glowing bulbs of happy memories, while others are dimly lit by moments of reflection. Just remember, every light and shadow adds depth to the party, making it uniquely yours.

Party Games: Pin the Tail on the Expectation

It's time for some fun and games! How about a round of "Pin the Tail on the Expectation"? Blindfolded, navigating the maze of societal pressures, can you pin your hopes and dreams in just the right spot? It's trickier than it sounds, but oh, the laughter it sparks!

The Buffet of Coping Mechanisms

This isn't your ordinary spread of sandwiches and quiches. It's a buffet of coping mechanisms:

- **Binge-Watching Delights:** Sometimes, losing yourself in a series is the perfect way to find yourself.

- **Treats of Tranquility:** Mindful meditation bites, anyone? Or perhaps a slice of yoga relaxation?

- **Desserts of Distraction:** From puzzles to paint-by-numbers, indulge in activities that keep the mind engaged and the heart light.

Toasting to Tomorrow: The Optimism Cocktail

Raise your glass (or teacup) and let's toast to the future. It's a blend of hope, a dash of dreams, shaken (not stirred) with resilience. It might taste a bit peculiar at first but give it a sip; the aftertaste is pure joy.

Wrapping Up: The Goodie Bag of Wisdom

No party's complete without a goodie bag! As you leave, take along a bag filled with wisdom, memories, and maybe a rubber duck (because why not?). It's a little reminder that even after the music fades and the guests leave, the journey, the lessons, and the strength remain.

Trauma's After-Party: RSVP to Resilience & Remember to Dial-a-Shrink!

Let's get real for a moment. Facing trauma is like trying to eat spaghetti with a spoon – it's messy, complicated, and there's a high probability of sauce-related mishaps. But if there's one thing spaghetti has taught us, it's to twirl through it all and, most importantly, never give up, especially when there's a meatball (or a life goal) at the end of it.

The "Oops, Did I Do That?" Moments

Life after trauma can come with a few unexpected spills and trips – both emotionally and metaphorically. You might find yourself crying over a commercial featuring a particularly moving appliance or laughing at the sheer absurdity of a situation. It's okay. Embrace the unpredictability, and always have a napkin handy!

The 24/7 Help Hotline (And We're Not Talking Pizza Delivery)

While the number for the nearest pizza place is essential (hello, comfort food!), it's just as crucial to have your therapist or helpline on speed dial. Remember, seeking help is like calling tech support for your soul. Sure, you might be put on hold or asked if you've tried turning your emotions off and on again, but these professionals are there to help troubleshoot your feelings.

Life's Rollercoaster: The Ups, Downs, and Loop-de-Loops

After trauma, life can feel like a rollercoaster designed by a caffeine-fueled toddler. There are sudden dips, unexpected rises, and the occasional loopy loop. But hey, even on the wildest rides, remember to scream with gusto, enjoy the thrill, and maybe, just maybe, throw your hands in the air!

The Mental Health Toolkit: Now with Added Glitter!

Think of mental health as your personal DIY project. Sometimes, you need to sand down rough edges. Other times, you're adding a splash of color. Don't be afraid to break out your toolkit. And if therapy is a wrench, humor is definitely the glitter – it makes everything brighter and sticks around, often in unexpected places! "Grabbed some nuggets of wisdom from this book? Toss 'em in your life toolkit, right next to that emergency glitter!"

In Conclusion: The Comeback Tour

Trauma might've been a tough act, but your comeback tour will be legendary. The key is never giving up on the main star of the show: YOU. Whether it's seeking help, leaning on loved ones, or laughing in the face of adversity, you're poised for an encore that's worth every standing ovation. So, here's to the fighters, the chucklers, and everyone dancing in the rain. Remember, every storm passes, and there's always a rainbow (or at least a good umbrella) waiting for you on the other side. Rock on, resilient warrior!

About the Author

Bernice Walker is a Nationally Board-Certified Counselor with a robust 14 years of hands-on experience. She has delicately woven the threads of understanding, empathy, and expertise into every interaction with her clients. Bernice's deep-rooted commitment to mental well-being is evident in her unwavering dedication to those she serves.

As a trauma specialist, Bernice has seen the profound depths of human resilience and the power of transformation. She firmly believes that amidst the weighty chapters of pain and struggle, there's a space for humor, light, and recovery. It's this belief that inspired her debut work, 'I Survived Trauma Now What..'. Through this book, Bernice aims to showcase that even in the darkest corners of trauma, a chuckle or a guffaw can be the very bridge that leads to healing.

Outside the therapy room, Bernice continues her quest for knowledge and growth, often engaging in community outreach and attending workshops to further hone her skills. With 'I Survived Trauma Now What..', she embarks on a new journey, extending her therapeutic touch beyond her practice and into the hands and hearts of readers everywhere.

Made in the USA
Coppell, TX
29 November 2023